For fun music, activities, and crafts, please use QR code reader app on your your smartphone and scan this code, or follow ArtsKindred on Instagram @ArtsKindred
www.ArtsKindred.com

A Day In The Life Of A Kid

CIRCUS IS FUN FOR EVERYONE!

written by Anetta Kotowicz
illustrated by Nina Ezhik

artsKinDreS
2020 New York

Aahhh, good night my dearest friends,
Huggie-hug!
The clock struck chime!
Playing tricks all through the day,
Let's now hushhh...
It's cuddle time!

TWOOT-twoot THUMP!

Ellie, is it you?

Trumpeting our friendship ROMP
Sounding high and sounding low:
TWOOT-twoot, THUMP!
    CLAP-clap, STOMP!
I'll take you to my favorite show!

Look!
A man up twenty feet,

Marks his way with CLICK click CLICKs,

Every step he makes a beat,
High-five him as he walks on sticks!

BOOM! BOOM! BOOM! BOOM!
BOOM! We start the grand parade,
TWOOT-TWOOT, TOOM-ti-ti TOOM,
Ellie blows as brass is played!

Clap-clap, STOMP!
Clap-clap, STOMP!
This is our friendship ROMP!

The acrobats all take their START,
Towers, stunts,
and tricky splits,
The monkeys love these works of art
With OOHS, AAHS,
and cheering fits!

Clap-clap, STOMP!
Clap-clap, STOMP!
This is our
friendship ROMP!

Now,
some SILENCE if you please!
Slowly, so he never fails,
(Hedgehogs,
STOP your shaking knees!)
A man lays on a bed
of nails.

Look up there!
Up in the sky!
Zooming with a whooshing ZOOP,

Parrots watch! Trapezes fly
While acrobats swing Loop-ty LOOP!

Clap-clap, STOMP!
Clap-clap, STOMP!
This is our friendship ROMP!

Spotlight high!
Don't even sigh!
Tightrope walkers' act is great,
Squirrels whisper count:
1 – 2 – ...
3 – 4 –

Audience shouts: **GIVE US MORE!**
They just love us on the floor,
But I heard the next act plans,
I was speechless,
Made me wonder,
Why...?

Is this right? Is this wrong?
You're my friends. You aren't? Do you?
Maybe someone helps along?
Ellie waits.
Choose what to do!

What just happened with our show? That's the way you'd like it to go?

Trembling heart,
I'm ready to shout:
Clap-clap, STOMP!
... and Ellie's OUT!

善待

LET'S BE FRIENDS

BĄDŹ NASZYM GŁOSEM!

Softest clap-claps cross the air,
Stomps then join, and tide goes on
Clap-clap, STOMP! Clap-clap, STOMP!
Join us in our
friendship ROMP!

SHOW US ♥

НАМ НЕ БАЙДУЖЕ

Leave the past! LOVE will last!

The ringmaster comes
with his swing-swang moves,
To Ellie proudly smiles in turn:

"When mistakes are made
WE FIX THEM FAST!
Joking friends,
come, join, and learn"

TWOOT-twoot, THUMP! CLAP-clap, STOMP!
Let's NOT STOP our FRIENDSHIP ROMP!

Twisty moves, and folky grooves,
We are grateful and impressed!
Wiggling snakes uncoil and clap,
All while dressed
in Sunday best.

CLAP-clap, STOMP!
BOOM-boom, STOMP!
This is our friendship ROMP!

Vanishing chameleons turn
Their eyes to us, and give a wink.
Clap-clap, STOMP! Clap-clap, STOMP!
This is our friendship ROMP!

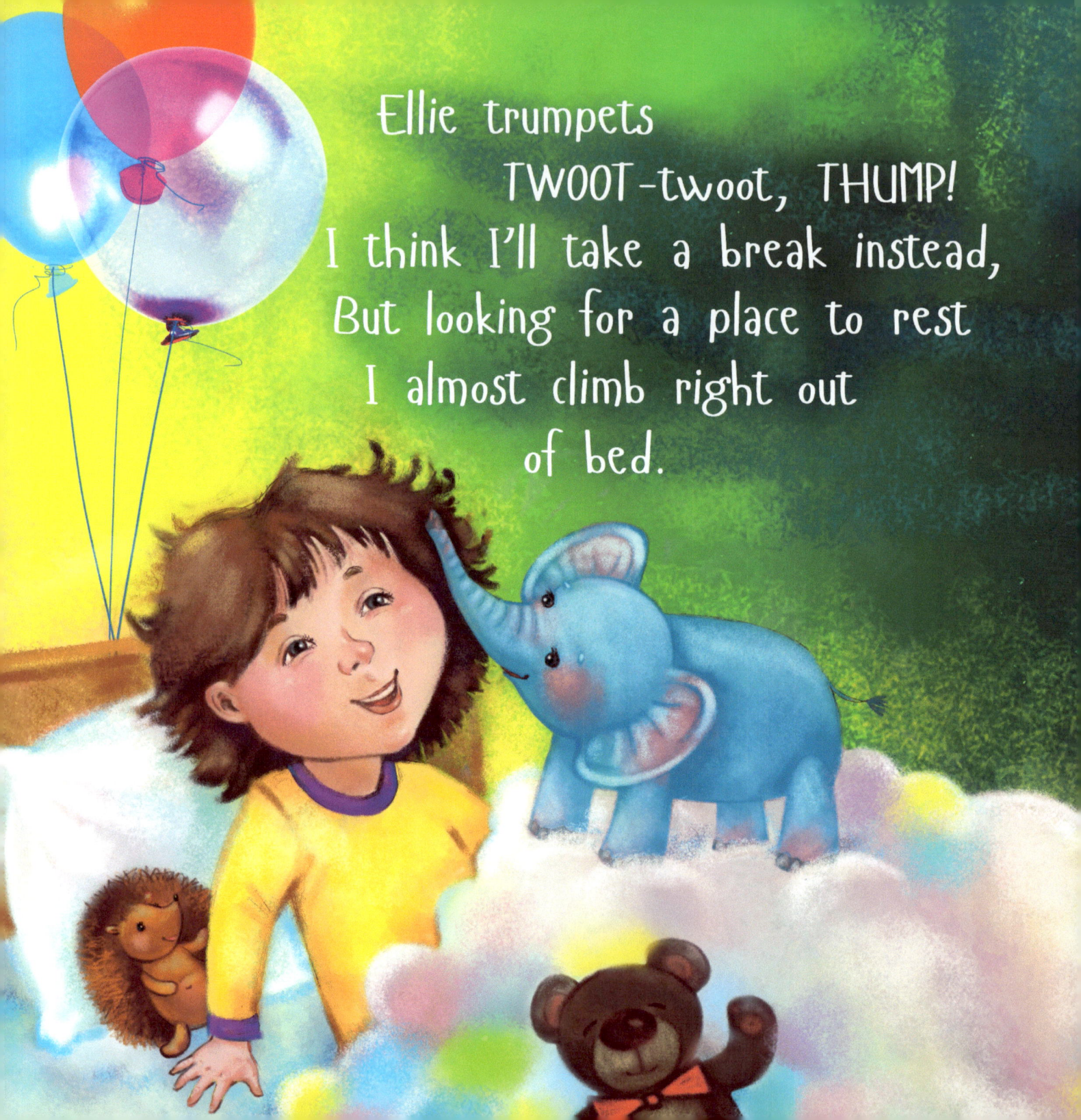

Ellie trumpets
 TWOOT-twoot, THUMP!
I think I'll take a break instead,
But looking for a place to rest
I almost climb right out
 of bed.

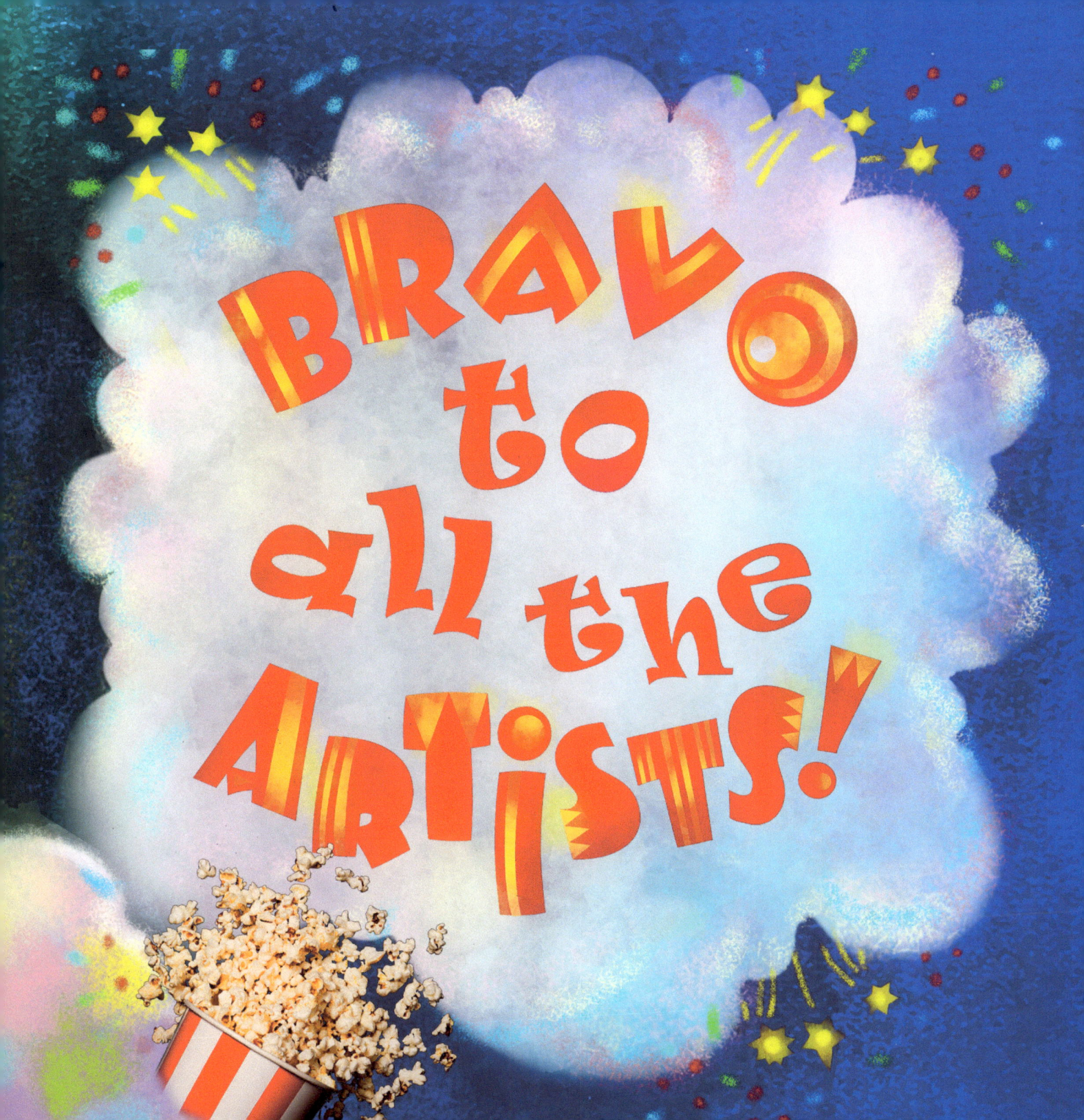

Awww... Is it over?
Well... My circus dream is, but we have so much more to explore.
Check out other books filled with songs, music and new outdoor adventures.
Visit www.ArtsKindred.com for books, music, coloring pages and activity ideas.

IG Follow @ArtsKindred

If you enjoyed this book, please support us
leaving your review on Amazon.com